PRAISE POWER

PRAISE POWER

Words of Inspiration, Power and Devotion

Michael Welsh

Praise Power

Copyright © 2021 by Michael Welsh. All rights reserved.

No part of this publication may be reproduced, stored in a retrieval system or transmitted in any way by any means, electronic, mechanical, photocopy, recording or otherwise without the prior permission of the author except as provided by USA copyright law.

The opinions expressed by the author are not necessarily those of URLink Print and Media.

1603 Capitol Ave., Suite 310 Cheyenne, Wyoming USA 82001
1-888-980-6523 | admin@urlinkpublishing.com

URLink Print and Media is committed to excellence in the publishing industry.

Book design copyright © 2021 by URLink Print and Media. All rights reserved.

Published in the United States of America

Library of Congress Control Number: 2021908967
ISBN 978-1-64753-791-3 (Paperback)
ISBN 978-1-64753-792-0 (Hardback)
ISBN 978-1-64753-793-7 (Digital)

01.03.21

A DAY IN EDEN

What is this perfect motion of the stars all out in space?
What does it say about creation? Are these the physics of God's grace?

Is it the heart of the Creator reaching out to fallen man?
Who is this great Designer...infinite measure in His hand?

Who has combined the elements comprising mountains, seas and air?
Meteorologists and geologists stand aghast at a world so fair!

Tectonic plates form but a crust for infernal regions far below.
Intense thermal activity is oft revealed by lava's flow.

Yet still the pines so gently wave. Bright fish in tropic waters fare.
A perfect balance fills the Earth, and beauty beyond compare!

Oceanographers and ecologists still discover harmony
In spite of man who spoils it while seeking destiny.

Astronomers long have wrestled with man's place in the universe.
Now physicists quote philosophers in science but somewhat versed.

But One who indwells the cosmos still transcends all He has made.
The Maker to redeem the Earth, Himself the price has paid...

And it seemed the very sun that day failed the Darkness to resist...
Still nature's critical mass was found in Him of Whom all things consist!

In Eden's day God's glorious radiance covered man, and God by man was known.
But man, choosing freely, sinned where the favor of God was shown.

Once-regal man was fallen, in sin and darkness bound...
But by grace, the Savior, His "treasure in a field" has found!

So creation, though quite glorious, has even yet a brighter day...
When God's sons reign in the Earth again...what then shall the agnostics say?

Mike Welsh
02-25-01

A SPIRITUAL THING

A spiritual thing today has begun
And shall echo for ages to come
To fulfill what's been spoken in word and in song,
In the Spirit prevailing as one.

For the warfare we face in the challenge of work and our
Victories in days just ahead
Have begun here and now, so let's water the seed
For soon we shall have what we said.

For we've faithfully spoken what's strong in our hearts
And it's just a matter of time.
As we diligently tend to the natural things,
It won't be too long 'till we find...

That the Lord and Creator of all that exists,
Who spoke and brought life into being,
Is also High Priest of confessions today
And he's Lord of these spiritual things!

Mike Welsh
12/19/03

APPRECIATE

How good we had it...
This I'd like to hear!
What was that blissful state?
A favorite bygone year?

Appreciation is a thankful key
Truly the best things in our lives
Are free!

So recollect as you reflect
Sweet friendships in your story,
And service given to Christ the King!
Cast crowns before His glory!

Mike Welsh
2/2/06

ATONEMENT AND GRACE

Hope through atonement was wrought
As the sacrifice yearly was brought,

For the blood of a bull, goat or lamb
Was the symbol of salvation's plan.

What this type and this shadow foresaw
Was a grace going deeper than law;

For the One which the type pointed to
The work of redemption did do

When Jesus provided the way,
Through His blood, for remission today.

And salvation's grace by redemption begun
Surpassed the atonements completed in One

Who as Scapegoat took sin although sinless and right,
Bore it's curse and has surely shown a great light;

For by grace and great kindness, the Creator of all
Again purchased the race which was lost in the fall

When the body began dying; the conscience was torn;
The mind and emotions...soon dejected, forlorn...

And the spirit of man, stained by sin had no right
To preside in the Earth and to walk in the light.

But as skins couldn't cover man's shame or his fear,
Hell's best couldn't hinder a new king's entrance here.

The first time as a babe, and then King and Priest...
And next as the "Lord of All" triumphant o'er the Beast.

All the world shall witness His coming in the air,
And His march through the gates of Jerusalem fair!

Jesus walks on the Earth and the saints start to sing...
"His Holiness: how glorious" and that eternal theme:

And we'll sing that "The theme of redemption lives still!
In our hearts and our lives, Christ the whole man has healed!"

Mike Welsh
10-25-00

BE PRAISED!

How rightly may your Name be praised,
O' Mighty One of old?
For only in the heart of man
is birthed a praise so bold!

How rightly may your Name be praised?
Most High, yet ever near...
Thou standest in a righteous place
The cries of faith to hear!

How rightly may your Name be praised,
O' Mighty One of old?
When shall redeemed ones tread with thee
On streets of purest gold?

How rightly may your Name be praised,
Fine Prince dispelling fear?
Both judging and dispensing grace,
Thy throne so bright and clear!

How rightly may your Name be praised,
Returning King of all?
Hear fervent prayer, victorious cries...
Thy chosen at the wall.

How rightly may your Name be praised,
O' Mighty One of old?
May yet thy counsel, peace and joy
Draw masses to thy fold!

How rightly may your Name be praised,
Great Healer ever sure!
To praise thee now, restore our souls...
To thee, forever pure!

Mike Welsh
1-25-10

BEAR THE PEN

Revelation, a concept, and then a short phrase...
A poem, inspired, Heaven's anthem to raise!

A pen and a paper, though but instruments plain,
With a word from the Master, can soothe away pain!

Just a moment's reflection, inspiration can bring.
Do the work of the psalmist! Thrill the heart of the King!

Bear the pen, for it's mightier far than the sword
To uniquely bring glory to eternity's Lord!

Mike Welsh
3-26-10

BELIEVE THE BEST

Believe the best of others and you'll often be correct.
Another's reputation is a thing we should protect!

So if some news of scandal you should perchance to hear,
Please lift your fellow Christian up! Petition for God's ear!

In doing so, the tide will turn if they were ill-inclined...
And you'll put on the mind of Christ! So bear this truth in mind...

Believe the best and intercede in faith and fervent prayer.
You'll find God's love perfected as another's pains you bear!

So you'll delight the heart of God... and find that you are blessed.
Believe the best of others! Trust in God and pass the test!

Mike Welsh
3-31-10

BIRTH OF MAN

At the dawn and creation of all that men see,
From a higher dimension was spoken, "Light be!"

A vacuum, the canvas between nature and Spirit,
Set the stage for words spoken...even now I can hear it.

"Light be!" he commanded, in authority risen
Over darkness and night, shining forth as a prism.

The creator of cosmos, with a personal touch,
Splashed the worlds into being, never calling it much...

But behold, it was GOOD and it gladdened his soul
When His crowning achievement made creation whole.

He called it a man, in the image of three!
A spirit, a soul and a body had he.

A 'mind in a body' other creatures God made.
But his man was a spirit that will not die nor fade.

After sin, man's dark soul found itself in a realm
Where enemy spirits could at times overwhelm.

But the Word was the power to redeem and to heal,
When man humbled himself at an altar to kneel.

Soon came a New Testament, to believers given...
Who believe that from death, their Savior is risen.

As the Word was the Light when creation began,
Now the Light of the Word brings completion to man.

And time is compressed into eternal NOW at the door of the spiritual realm
As time and space BEND at the Source of all light!
She's a great ship with Christ at the helm!

Mike Welsh
5/4/05

CHRIST IN US

Now that Christ is formed in us, we can minister grace;
His Spirit in us does the work.
Sacrificially giving of time, strength or wealth,
Our reward is much more than a 'perk.'

Now those touched by his grace will flow in that stream
Of anointing and peace from above.
With God's thoughts to fill us, and his purpose as ours,
There's no end to the power of his love!

Mike Welsh
3/19/04

DESTINY

Man reaches forth
To explore destiny

Predestined for glories
He cannot see.

Only by faith
In the God who lives

Can a man find all
He is to be ... and is!

Mike Welsh
4/26/00

DEVOTION

There's a fire of devotion that burns in my life,
And I oft must rekindle it's flame;
For how quickly and often distractions come
With worry, temptation or pain.

In your presence Lord, there's fullness of joy
And your perfect love casteth out fear.
As the fire of devotion burns long and burns sure,
Pain is eased, for it's your Word I hear!

So devotion will rise with a new, brighter flame
And purge away dross from this life.
For the Spirit-filled walk has a powerful way
Of defeating the power of strife!

And love will prevail as devotion's flame burns
For I'll worship, yes sing and praise too!
As your presence is felt, I'm assured of your love;
For the end of my worship is You!

Mike Welsh
5/24/04

EMMANUEL

In times we call 'antiquity'
    Came power to quell iniquity.

As we're embroiled in struggles here,
    From heaven has come God's
    Spirit dear...

Allaying fears, replacing dread...
    With joy and peace from
    Christ our Head.

This body's fitly joined and pure...
    In Him alone, our Promise sure.

Now sin is broken...tidings tell,
    Through Christ our Lord
    Emmanuel.

Mike Welsh
12/31/01

EXCELLENCE

Intensity and excellence are now at work in me.
The author of my faith also the finisher shall be!

Seeds planted in obedience and faith in days gone-by
Are germinating, breaking ground and soon shall touch the sky.

The Spirit's supernatural move shall bring newness of life.
The old shall fade, the new shall come, with power to dethrone strife.

The races shall agree as one and unity abound
For those who in the Book of Life find their names written down.

Now gone are days of doubt and lack and low-living as well;
For glorious is the reign of Christ! His kingdom news we tell!

Mike Welsh
11-14-03

FAIR HAVEN

O' frail bark afloat on the ocean of life
How will you chart your way?

Will you go wherever the wind carries you
Or hear what the stars have to say?

For creation so vast holds a compass that's true
Although safety and peace seem long gone.

In a moment of grace there's an unction divine
And a mandate for you to press on!

For somewhere ahead a safe harbor waits!
There you'll anchor in God's fair atoll

And rejoice when your wandering journeys are past.
You're at peace, still happy and whole!

Mike Welsh
07-02-03

GLORIFY

God's kids bring glory to Him best, not just with hands upraised,

but through the actions of our lives, the deeds of all our days.

Yet all expressions, we create, can God Most High appreciate!

When from the heart and true, our praise is more than what we do!

Our words alone can best describe to Him the glory we ascribe!

Still words alone utterly fail to take our hearts beyond the veil.

So dance and song must be brought in, releasing rivers from within.

And could the writer's pen reverse dark moods and counter Adam's curse?

Rejoice! Redemption is revealed! So give Him praise! Mankind is healed!

Mike Welsh
3-22-10

GRACE NEVER ENDING

Sultry and sullen the weather;
The routine's a monotonous grind;
Hard to see through the fog and the smog of each day...
To believe that this cloud's silver-lined.

Yet the pace and the rhythm of labor...
The commitments of toil that we find
Are the furnace yet forging our talents and roles;
Therein character always refined.

Can we reconcile natural wisdom
And the trappings of temporal life
With a nature still deeper that's calling
Like a spiritual harp and a fife?

It's a purpose that beckons us onward;
A knowing that somehow there's more...
Reason whispers "Creator...a Designer",
And then there's the door;

At the heart a continual knocking;
He politely and patiently waits.
The King of all Kings and Lord of all Lords;
Day-to-day must He find that He rates...

More than just a casual "thank you",
More than just a moment of praise;
It takes time and attention, meditation in fact,
To acknowledge Him in all of our ways.

And drawing aside from the cares of the day,
As emotions and senses are healed,
The dust of the world washed away from our feet,
In the Word is God's greatness revealed.

The awesome and infinite power
Of omnipotent God...Who is Light;
His power and greatness unending,
Putting forces of darkness to flight.

His ethereal, mystical Presence
Out beyond Earth's gossamer veil,
Gives a reason and rhyme to existence
Causing sadness and sorrow to pale.

And yet distance and time make no difference
The Person of Christ to avail.
He's a Friend sticking closer than family can do;
It's impossible that He can fail.

For as great and as awesome a God
As is found in the scriptures of old,
This compassionate personal ally
Is our Savior! The future He holds.

Mike Welsh
04-28-98

INVASION OF GRACE

The fool has said in his heart, "There's no God!"
Yet many think they point the way,
Through astrology making creation their god,
Just as millions have done to this day.

Whether Hindus or Buddhists or cults
With a million false-gods or just one,
There's a place and a time to focus upon
Rich or poor, of all races they come.

And in American culture
Where capitalism prevails
Even materialists, like you and me,
Can find "Jesus (it's true) never fails!"

Whether wickens or witches or Satanists,
Cult membership seems on the rise.
But a far greater movement has risen
Inclusive to those who are wise

Enough to acknowledge the price that was paid
On Golgotha, where Christ's blood was poured.
Prophetic fulfillment as God's Lamb was slain;
There's salvation now; "Jesus is Lord!"

Over all other spiritual forces
Of darkness, even "angels of light"
Who seduce and destroy many fools of this world
And would tempt us away from True Light.

But the True Light has come and He shines in our hearts
And His coming-again has grown near.
Now the saved are a witness, a message to you;
Turn to Jesus when His voice you hear!

Mike Welsh
04-28-98

LIFE WORTH LIVING

The blood Christ offered was real blood,
Not a symbol or token of pain,
But the essence of God's great redemption,
To cleanse away every sin stain.

God first shed blood for a covering for Eve,
And for Adam, both yet in the garden.
The results of their sin were addressed thereby;
God's covenant then foreshadowed sin's pardon.

Law said if by man another were killed,
Then turnabout, kill him...fair play.
Yet no man will ever Christ's death outdo,
For deliverance has come just that way.

He hung on a cross! God's righteous lamb died,
Israel's Passover happening then.
No greater love hath a man, He had said,
Than to lay down his life for his friends.

He was wounded for our transgressions;
He was bruised for our iniquities;
The chastisement of our peace was upon Him;
By His stripes we are healed, soothed and eased.

Remitted, not simply atoned-for,
Cancelled, not just carried away;
The words prophesied were fulfilled in full measure
By real blood shed for me on that day.

Because it was not just symbolic,
But historic in real space and time,
I face each new day with a conscience renewed
And a joy that's exclusively mine;

For the price Jesus paid for me legally there
And His victory o'er regions below
Confirm that my new life, in Him, is well-founded;
I've and entrance to Heaven I know.

And reign in this life...yes I can and I must!
I'm authority, grace and power given.
My penalty's been paid and the docket is clear.
Life's abundant, sin's gone; life again is worth living.

Mike Welsh
01-01-92

LORD I WOULD NOT BE PRAYERLESS

Lord, I would not be prayerless in this life, not one more day,
But seek that thing which pleases you. If there my heart could stay!

Why should I dwell on earthly things? Though work and rest must come,
I'll face the dawn; I'll praise your name with righteous garments on!

Lord, I would not be prayerless, but would consecration prove;
As words of faith transform this life, touched by the Spirit's move.

Lord, I would not be prayerless, but would intercede awhile;
And ever seek to do in life what makes your great heart smile!

Lord, I would not be prayerless, in a time a of darkest pain;
But there recall what you endured, and find heaven's refrain.

Lord, I would not be prayerless! In communion there's a rest.
I'll leave my cares and comfort find; you speak and I am blessed!

Mike Welsh
04-09-04

LOVE EYES

If eyes of Love are the eyes of God, then come Lord, see through me!
May eyes of faith and love set many captives free!

As Jesus' words of love and power would heal the halt and lame,
The evidence *showed* in his face; of why from heaven he came.

A love as strong as the love of God won't compromise or cease.
This love can calm the fiercest storms, restoring hearts with peace.

How glorious now the radiance from our hearts set aglow!
For joy and peace and love *abound* when his great love we know!

Mike Welsh
12-11-03

MARAH

(Bitter Waters Made Sweet Ex. 15:23)

Disappointment and hardship, although common to us all,
Are often cliffs, sheer and formidable, hence wonderment and awe.

So the heart of many is made to weep and cower there;
The Prince of Darkness tightens bonds and shackles of despair.

"Bitterness the pill to swallow" natural sages often say.
Placing blame and pointing fingers are the language of the day.

But a culture thus infected, filled with rancor and dismay
Are but pristine opportunities for miracles I say;

For the Father and the Holy Ghost, when working in my life,
Burst power forth upon the scene, replacing death and strife.

For when the Spirit manifests in His almighty way,
Perceived or unnoticed, soon peace and joy are underway.

And swiftly moving to the heart of matters so frustrating and intense,
Speak life and grace and blessing, soon dispatching Satan hence.

So the faint of heart are quieted; the strong are reassured.
For skill and strength come not from ease, but through hardships if endured.

Mike Welsh
01-04-00

O' WORK OF GOD

O' hinder not the work of God that He's begun in me...
For I'll yet testify of Him who hung upon the tree.

And more shall be than what has been of His great move and work.
The increase of His reign exceeds the skills of scribe and clerk.

This time of prayer today a move of grace shall usher-in.
His kingdom rules with power to quench iniquity and sin!

O' work of God continue-on in heart and mind and soul,
And find here, when work is done, a multitude made whole!

Mike Welsh
10-31-03

O' ROLLING STONE

How long now, o' rolling stone
Can you hinder 'heaven's door'
And hide the advent of my King
With keys of death, and more?

Not long will you, o' rolling stone
Stand defiant, as a fool
Who says, "there is no God"
Or that He's dead or 'pull the wool'

And so deceive, or twist the fact
That hell and death can't stand
When challenged by the risen Christ
Or by the blood-washed band.

For millions shall perceive the truth
That sin can't satisfy
And that a rolling stone, so set
Is nothing but a lie!

O' rolling stone, the Lord of all the earth
Victorious, draweth near!
You rocks that trembled three days prior
Again will quake and fear!

So best you fall or roll away
Forever from your place!
The Light of heaven has returned
With glory in His face!

A chance remains now, rolling stone,
That you may praise His name...
Creation cries until the day
All praise Him just the same!

So come Lord Jesus, till the soil
If stony hearts you see.
Create a garden fit for seeds
And bring lost souls to thee!

Mike Welsh
9/16/05

OLD TO NEW

An eye for an eye, a tooth for a tooth,
The law and commandments were stern;

A schoolmaster pointing the way out ahead
Ere God's grace we eventually learn.

Cursed as the snake Moses placed on a pole;
And those looking upon it were spared...

Our Scapegoat was finally made sin for us
Outside the gate...but who cared?

Three keys now are proof of His triumph
Over death, hell, the grave, and hell's host.

Today we rejoice in His resurrection power,
New life and the great Holy Ghost.

Mike Welsh
01-01-92

PEACE

Though politics fail...there reigns a Prince
Where in the land God's people dwell...

So often fraught with violence,
Still Peace will come to Israel.

Mike Welsh
5/26/07

PRAISE POWER

Today, the presence of the Lord our praise can usher-in!
This is the day of outpourings...the day of conquered sin!

Few in the past truly foresaw such things that God would do...
That gifts and callings from His hand would baptize me and you.

The day has come for mighty works as praise resounds on high...
A season of great power has come; the Savior draweth nigh.

The healer of the wounded heart, the lover of the soul
Shall tread down all our enemies. Messiah has control!

For what has been and what shall be are working in "the now."
By faith and worship enter-in...this kingdom with no end;

For as His presence fills the Earth,
We find our dearest friend!

Mike Welsh
11/19/03

RACE AND RIGHTEOUSNESS

Are we yet one in the Body of Christ or must we seek another day?
And have we yet so many things...on the altar we must lay?

Does prejudice rule the races when a family we should be?
Are others also mirrors to reveal lost parts of me?

And can we see the One who died, the races to redeem,
And walk in love and grace despite how different others seem?

Could Jews and gentiles, long at odds, be grafted to one tree?
Did not our Lord break down this wall in dying agony?

Was not this war finally won the day His side was riven?
Forever settled it shall be! His righteousness He's given!

If Christ paid such a price to bring all races to His throne,
To such great love would you respond and make your heart His home?

For as you do, His righteousness defeats the power of shame!
Self-doubt and anger, strife and fear will go in Jesus' name.

Emancipation of *all men*, a matter of the heart,
Was bought by Him who makes us one, restoring every part.

For mankind was *His* plan and joy, the Church not just His friend,
But now 'His Bride' we boldly stand, devoted to the end.

Mike Welsh
06-20-05

REDEMPTION OF SOULS

The redemption of souls is the finest thing this world as yet has known.
'Tis the kindest grace, the truest light that e're from heaven has shown.

Sin's evil plague that covered all men left them poor, ill-fated and blind;
But creation's great God perfected a plan to reconcile and restore mankind.

Earth, flora and fauna, all touched by the curse
And humanity too, even writers of verse

Have been stained by that fall and are hindered therein.
We would fain be restored, fellowship to begin

With the One whose Words brought all things into being
And would share untold beauty and blessings unseen

With the man that He loved and would die to restore.
But we hungrily strive, not satisfied, wanting 'more.'

Having sought, like a sickness epidemic in it's sweep,
Desire espouses greater hunger, never satisfaction's sleep.

But rest we can and rest we will when coming to the cross;
Responding to His remedy, count all our gains but loss.

We revel in the mystery: He died new life to give!
Innocence was punished and now the undeserving live.

Obedience our work...to admit our need for Him;
Forgiveness showed His grace...His pardon for our sin.

Our life in Him is spiritual. Our souls are set on fire.
Our sacrifice was offered once on death's official pyre.

"Eye for an eye" and "blood for blood," the law's demands would test.
But Christ, the anointed Lamb of God prevailed o'er Satan's best.

So all we have and all we need...embodied now in Him;
We live and move and have our being and victories can win!

Death and defeat and poverty, the curse of Adam's fall,
Were cancelled with our sin, guilt taken from us all.

"Whosoever" is the open door where enter the redeemed.
So heed the call, confessing Christ, then enter and believe!

    Mike Welsh
    04-26-00

REIGN OF PEACE

I've found the reign of peace and Kingdom power in my life
And in joyous, peaceful seasons find sweet respite from the strife;

Escaping the frustration found in daily situations
Fraught with fools and whining babies with their constant lamentations.

That hour of prayer and praise, devotion's true delight
Turns all my thoughts from worldly things...to walking in the light.

I face the truth of all that my Redeemer kinsman bought;
He ransomed those adopted ones who failed to do as taught.

Law's ten commandments proved us all unworthy like the rest.
But one pure, true, unblemished life prevailed and passed the test.

The Prince of Peace his title won by conquest, not default!
T'was not by merely giving-up he entered death's cold vault...

Where Lucifer who long has stood defiant as heaven's foe
Was made to pass beneath the yoke where vanquished armies go.

"Captivity led captive," in humiliation led;
Fulfilling ancient prophecy, Christ bruised the Serpent's head.

The trap was set, the scene was played, the scriptures tell the story;
Hell, if knowing redemption's song, would spare the "Lord of Glory!"

For by becoming "sin for us" and bearing all our sin
As Zion's scapegoat long ago, now outcasts are brought in.

Yes, grafted-in through faith…not works of keeping law,
Now even gentiles shun the curse brought on by Adam's fall.

So Christ has fought, the battle won. He came the price to pay.
With grace and joy our freedom bought. Faith brought a brighter day!

Mike Welsh
02-04-01

THE SHOUT

There's a shout in the house and a shout in the field,
An anointing of glory on both;
For the King will sustain those he died to redeem,
And is risen our hearts to betroth!

The creator of all is the 'lover of souls,'
Ever knowing what life may portend;
So keep singing His praise! Keep a shout in your heart!
Keep the victory...be strong to the end!

And faithfully serve with a shout in the house!
In the field make His victories known;
For the grace of our God, as His word has foretold,
Will let millions make Jesus their own.

Mike Welsh
06-05-04

THE SHROUD

Speak o' folded napkin in a sepulcher now bare. What say you now
Of Him whose head of late has rested there?

Will you yet speak of victory won from dark regions below?
For Death and Hell now vanquished leave all humans free to go.

And testify completion of deliverance by Him who bled,
His body bruised for iniquities, for strife thorns pierced His head.

He served the Church, completing all God's redemptive plan foreknew.
Powers of darkness, without light, couldn't grasp what He would do.

He kept the feast of Passover, Himself the Paschal Lamb,
Fulfilling types and prophecies, did what no mortal can.

WHY are you folded, napkin? ... because your work is finished too?
You tried to shroud the face of God, but glorious light shone through!

Remember, folded napkin, you can never veil the One
Whose grace and glory forever shall outshine the brightest sun.

The human hands that folded you, still pierced but glorified,
Will never bleed, but always heal the ones for whom He died.

United now, the Body of Christ fulfills His will on Earth...
To spread the gospel of His love and grant men heaven's worth!

Mike Welsh
5/10/03

TORCH FIRE

In days gone by, the Lord has set a good degree in store
For those who walk those hallowed halls, believing there is more.

Where mediocrity has failed, now excellence must prove
A new day and bright future calls and keeps them on the move.

Not stagnant, but a flowing stream, with rivers from within
To water where they sowed in faith and harvest souls of men.

For in this day and season now, outpourings have begun!
So walk in light, child of the day! You've yet to see the sun.

In righteousness He rises. In this new season stay!
Continue for you've well begun! His Spirit lights your way.

Your torches burn so keep them bright! Be strong and never sway,
For many live where light is dim and you can show the way!

Mike Welsh
11/19/03

WHAT HEALING STREAM!

What healing stream, engulfing me,
Now flows from Calvary's hill?

What ever-potent force behind
That Nazarene speaks still!

What healing stream, engulfing me,
Flows yet from Calvary?

What words delivered those like me
Held by iniquity.

What healing stream flows from the cross
And sweet communion gives!

What multitudes now testify...
Our Lord is One Who lives!!

What healing stream, engulfing me,
Prosperity does bring!

What joy has come into this heart
So often made to sing.

What healing stream, forgiving me,
Has healed a sinful man,

And brought a greater knowledge of
God's all-embracing plan.

What healing stream, still flowing, calls
To all who hear and bow.

And transformed by accepting Christ,
Find destiny starts NOW!

Mike Welsh
7/8/06

WITH ME

Thank you Lord that you are with me...
Ever present, ever strong!

You are with me in your strength and power,
through the night and all day long.

O' gentle savior, you've not passed me
Nor deferred to hear by call!

You've promised never to forsake me,
But keep safe and give me all!

Mike Welsh
8/13/05

YOUR BEAUTY

Lord Jesus now your beauty has become my heart's desire...
And all the world's distractions are but pebbles in the mire.

Lord, may my love for you be one that ever flows...
To give the treasures of my heart and all my spirit knows.

For you Lord Jesus, ever wise, will come when time is right,
Restoring existential things with righteousness and light.

Lord Jesus may my heart long always after you...
Until your Kingdom work is done and all that's left is you.

Eternity awaits, and yet I'll worship, praise and sing.
May highest praises flow to thee...our Lord, and Christ and King!

Mike Welsh
1-25-10

www.ingramcontent.com/pod-product-compliance
Ingram Content Group UK Ltd.
Pitfield, Milton Keynes, MK11 3LW, UK
UKHW022219230426
12048UKWH00016BA/933